CONTENTS

WHO WERE THE AZTECS?

The Aztec people, led by their emperor, Moctezuma, ruled over a huge, rich **empire**. This empire was in the land that is now Mexico. Their capital, Tenochtitlan, was one of the world's largest cities. In 1519, the Spanish attacked and destroyed the Aztec Empire. They also destroyed evidence that would have told us how the Aztecs lived.

Before the Aztecs

Civilizations existed in Mexico long before the Aztec empire. The Olmecs lived in Mexico from about 1300 BC. They were skilled **sculptors** and artists.

This is a map of the land that is now Mexico. It shows where the people who were there before the Aztecs lived.

A Mixtec earring
This gold earring was made by the Mixtec people. They were skilled at making gold jewellery.

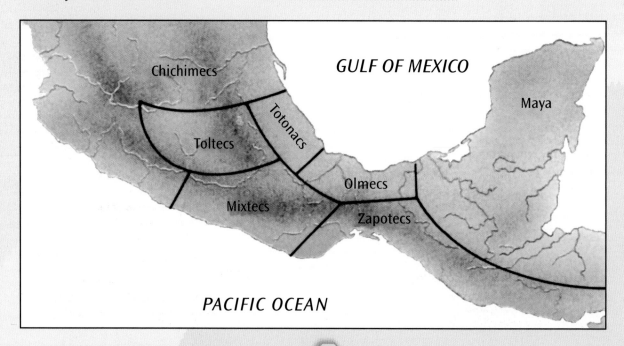

Chichimecs

GULF OF MEXICO

Maya

Totonacs

Toltecs

Olmecs

Mixtecs

Zapotecs

PACIFIC OCEAN

Revised and updated

Understanding People In The Past
The AZTECS

ROSEMARY REES

Heinemann
LIBRARY

www.heinemann.co.uk/library

Visit our website to find out more information about **Heinemann Library** books.

To order:

 Phone ++44 (0)1865 888066

 Send a fax to ++44 (0)1865 314091

 Visit the Heinemann Bookshop at www.heinemann.co.uk/library to browse our catalogue and order online.

First published in Great Britain by Heinemann Library, Halley Court, Jordan Hill, Oxford OX2 8EJ, part of Harcourt Education.
Heinemann is a registered trademark of Harcourt Education Ltd.

Editorial: Clare Lewis and Katie Shepherd
Design: Michelle Lisseter and Damco Solutions Ltd
Picture research: Hannah Taylor
Production: Helen McCreath

Originated by Dot Gradations Ltd
Printed and bound in China by WKT Company Ltd

13-digit ISBN: 978 0 431 07791 8 (hb)
10 09 08 07 06
10 9 8 7 6 5 4 3 2 1

13-digit ISBN: 978 0 431 07809 0 (pb)
11 10 09 08 07
10 9 8 7 6 5 4 3 2 1

British Library Cataloging in Publication Data
Rees, Rosemary, 1942-
The Aztecs. - 2nd ed. - (Understanding People in the Past)
972'.018
A full catalogue record for this book is available from the British Library.

Acknowledgments
The author and publisher are grateful to the following for permission to reproduce copyright material:
Ferdinand Anton, pp. 20; Bodleian Library, pp. 10 top, 11, 13 bottom, 14-17, 28, 30 top, 36, 42, 43 bottom, 45, 46, 48; C. M. Dixon, pp. 7 top, 33 bottom; E. T. Archive, pp. 57; Werner Forman Archive, pp. 4, 5, 6 bottom, 7 bottom, 8 bottom, 9, 10, 13, 18, 19, 20, 22, 23, 26, 27, 28, 29 bottom, 31 top, 32, 33 top, 37, 39, 40, 47, 49, 53, 59 top; Alan Hutchison Library, pp. 34, 35 top; Mexican Embassy, p. 59 bottom; Marion and Tony Morrison, p. 44; Nick Saunders/Barbara Heller Archive, p. 6 top; Salmer, p. 54; Syndication International, pp. 24, 30 bottom, 52 top, 53.
Cover photograph © Werner Forman Archive / British Museum, London.

The publishers would like to thank Dr. Elizabeth Baquedano for her advice on the content of this book.

Every effort has been made to contact copyright holders of any material reproduced in this book. Any omissions will be rectified in subsequent printings if notice is given to the publisher.

Some words are shown in bold, **like this**. You can find out what they mean by looking in the glossary.

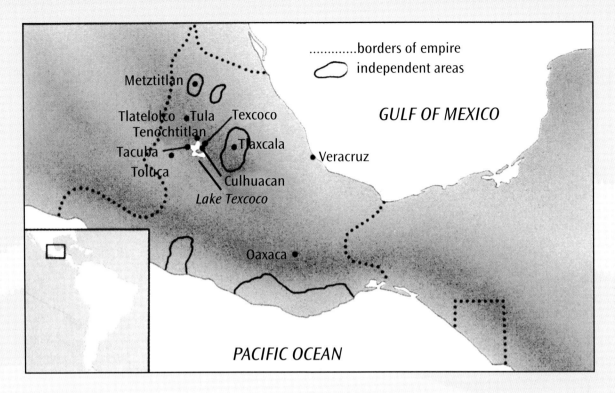

Metztitlan

Tlatelolco • Tula Texcoco
Tenochtitlan
Tacuba • Tlaxcala
Toluca
Culhuacan
Lake Texcoco

Oaxaca •

Veracruz •

GULF OF MEXICO

............borders of empire
independent areas

PACIFIC OCEAN

This map shows the Aztec Empire in 1519.

The Mayas of the Classic period lived in Mexico between AD 300 and AD 900. They were among the first people in Mexico to use picture writing called **glyphs**. The Toltecs settled in Mexico between AD 900 and AD 1150. Ruins of their buildings tell us they were great architects. When the Toltec empire collapsed, other tribes began to move into the area. The last tribe to arrive was the Aztecs.

At first the Aztecs had no land. In 1325 they settled on an island in the middle of Lake Texcoco. They built their capital city, Tenochtitlan, there. It became one of the biggest cities in the world. Within 200 years the Aztecs controlled an empire that stretched from the Atlantic to the Pacific coasts.

The Temple of the Warriors
*This **temple** was built by the Maya-Toltec. When the Aztecs built their temples, they copied some of the details from Toltec temples.*

HOW DO WE KNOW ABOUT THE AZTECS?

We know about the Aztecs and how they lived because we can look at things from their time that still exist today. We can look at the ruins of their buildings. We can look at smaller things such as pottery and jewellery. We can look at the pictures they made. These **artefacts** – things made by people – are sometimes buried deep in the ground. **Archaeologists** are people who are trained to **excavate** and uncover ruins of buildings and towns. They dig carefully and make drawings and take photographs of everything they uncover. They collect everything they find. They use this evidence to explain how the Aztecs lived and what happened to them.

Templo Mayor in Mexico City
This temple stood in the square in the middle of Tenochtitlan. It was a temple to the gods Huitzilopochtli and Tlaloc. Archaeologists uncovered it.

The ruins of Teotihuacan
No one knows which tribe of people built this city in about AD 200. Archaeologists and historians think that the Aztecs copied the layout of Teotihuacan when they built Tenochtitlan.

Archaeology in Mexico

The Aztecs lived in a country that is now called Mexico. Mexico City is the capital of Mexico. It is built on top of the ruins of Tenochtitlan. When a new subway station was built in Mexico City, the builders discovered old ruins. They called in archaeologists, who said that the ruins had once been an Aztec temple. It was the temple of the Aztec God of the Wind, Ehecatl-Quetzalcoatl.

Archaeologists excavated cities that were lived in long before the time of the Aztecs. They found artefacts that were much like Aztec artefacts. This tells us that the Aztecs used some of the ideas of earlier cultures.

Aztec pottery
The top picture is of a child's rattle. The bottom picture is of small pottery stamps. They were dipped in paint and used to print patterns on faces.

HISTORY IN PICTURES AND WORDS

Aztec writing

When the Aztecs wanted to write something they used little pictures, not words. These pictures are called glyphs. Each glyph was always drawn in the same way so everyone knew what the writer wanted to say. A footprint meant travel. A scroll meant speech. A shield and arrows meant war. Important people were drawn larger than people who were less important. Aztec **scribes** painted glyphs on to a kind of paper called **amatl**. The pages were joined together in a long zigzag.

An Aztec book is called a **codex**. These books tell us about Aztec history, prayers, calendars, taxes, and farming.

Aztec glyphs
This glyph shows the Fire Serpent marrying a flower. It means "the wind".

A codex
An Aztec book is called a codex. The plural of codex is codices.

Spanish writers

In 1519 soldiers from Spain, led by Hernán Cortés, invaded the Aztec Empire and defeated the Aztecs. People from Spain went to live in the newly conquered land. Spanish priests taught the Aztecs about Christianity. Some priests tried to find out more about the Aztecs and their way of life.

Father Bernadino de Sahagún arrived in New Spain, as the land was called, in 1529. He learned the Aztec language, Nahuatl, and talked to the Aztec leaders. Later he wrote a book called *General History of the Things in New Spain*. He wrote it in Spanish and Nahuatl. Friar Diego Durán was another Spanish priest. He wrote three books about Aztec history.

The problem with histories of the Aztecs is knowing what to believe. Much of what the Aztecs wrote about their own history was based on legends and is not absolutely true. Spanish writers tried to show that the Aztecs were uncivilized, and this is not true either. It is important to remember who was writing and how they got their information.

A statue of the god Quetzalcoatl
The god is carrying a load of corn on his back. A long strap goes around his forehead. This gives us an idea about how the Aztecs carried heavy loads.

AZTEC GOVERNMENT

The Aztecs were ruled by kings. When a king died, the **nobles**, priests, and warriors chose a new king. The new ruler was always from the same family as the dead king. Aztec kings had strong control over their empire. There were many wars and so the king had to be a clever soldier.

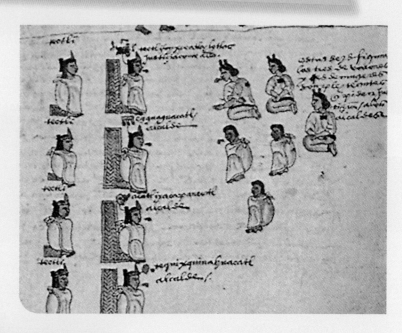

Crime and punishment

This picture from a codex shows an Aztec trial. The six people on the right are asking for justice from the judges on the left. An Aztec punishment might be piercing the guilty prisoner with cactus spines or taking away his land. Thieves were stoned or hanged. Prisoners could appeal to the Woman Snake or the Emperor if they did not agree with their punishment.

The headdress of Moctezuma

The Emperor Moctezuma wore this headdress. It was made from precious stones and feathers from the quetzal bird.

The most important person after the king was a man called the Woman Snake. He was in charge of law and order and collecting taxes. There was a small **council** of four nobles that gave the king advice. There was a larger council called the **tlatocan** that included tax collectors, judges, and scribes. They discussed things such as laws, whether the laws should be changed, and how much tax everyone should pay.

The calpulli family group

Every Aztec was a member of a **calpulli**. This was a clan or group of families that were related to each other. Calpullis organized the towns and villages in which they lived. The calpullis owned the land but were under the strict control of the king and the nobles. Each calpulli had a leader called a calpullec. His job was to see that the land was farmed properly and that **tributes** were paid on time. He had to make sure that the calpulli provided enough workers for the nobles. The nobles became more and more powerful after the 1420s as the Aztec empire grew larger.

A tribute list
The Aztecs made the people that they conquered pay tribute to them. This is a list of the tribute to be paid by 22 towns in the Tochtepec area. The towns had to send this amount of tribute to the Aztecs every year. What do you think they had to send?

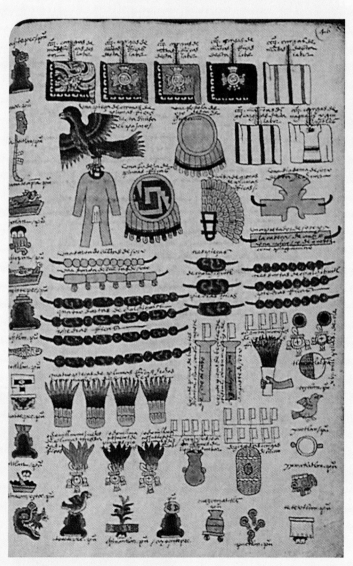

WHAT WERE THE AZTECS' CLOTHES LIKE?

The Aztecs thought it was important to know if a person's position in society was high or low. People's rank showed in the way they dressed. There were four main groups in Aztec society: nobles, commoners, **merchants**, and **slaves**. Commoners were ordinary people, such as farmers and craft workers. Slaves were people who were too poor to pay their tributes or live off the land.

The rules of dress

Only nobles were allowed to wear sandals and brightly coloured cloaks made from cotton. Commoners had to wear rough cloth. They were not allowed to wear anything that came below their knees.

Jnic v. parrapho ipan mitoa imzquintla month minedbichioaya mtlatoque ioā mcioapipiltin.

Aztec clothes
The man on the right is a nobleman. We know this because he wears a cloak that falls below his knees and he has sandals on his feet. Do you think the woman is from a noble family?

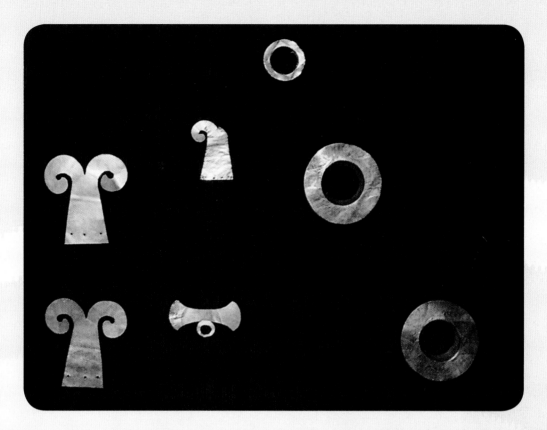

The Aztecs grew cotton and maguey plants and spun the fibres into thread. Every Aztec woman could weave the thread into cloth. They coloured the cloth with natural dyes made from plants, shellfish, and insects. Most Aztec clothes were lengths of cloth. The cloth could be wrapped around their bodies to make skirts, **loin cloths**, or cloaks. Cloaks were very important. The embroidery on the cloaks showed what the owner's job was. Aztecs who were brave in battle had special cloaks. A warrior who captured two prisoners was given a cloak with an orange border. Cloaks were given as tributes and were used for trading.

Gold jewellery for clothing and ears
Aztec men and women pierced their ears to wear jewellery or decorated their clothes with it.

Learning to weave
This picture from a codex shows a mother teaching her daughter to weave. Glyphs like these are all that remain to tell us what the Aztecs wore. All the actual cloth and clothes have rotted away.

FAMILY LIFE

When a man and a woman got married, the calpulli gave them a plot of land. They grew food on this land. When they had children and needed to grow more food, they asked the calpullec for more land. Every family had to work for the capullec and give him some of their crops. If a family did not do a good job of farming the land, the capullec took it away and gave it to another family who needed it.

An Aztec wedding
This picture of an Aztec wedding was drawn by Aztecs. The bride and groom are sitting together on a mat at the top of the picture. Their cloaks are tied together. This shows that they are now tied together as husband and wife.

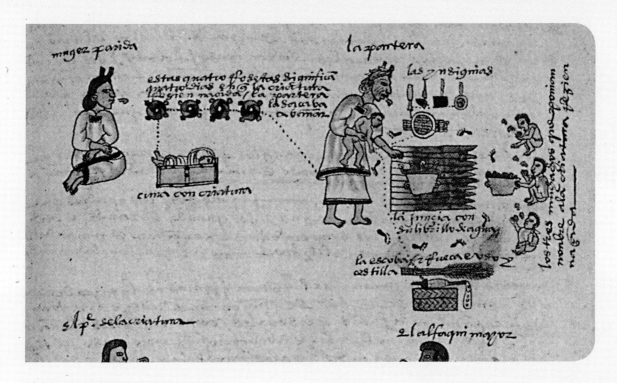

The first days in a baby's life
On the left of the picture is a mother talking to her baby. We know
that the baby is four days old because there are four rosettes above the
cradle. The midwife who helped the woman when the baby was born
is in the middle of the picture. She is taking the baby to be washed.

Marriage

Aztec parents arranged the marriages of their children. When a boy was about 20 years old, his father organized a feast and found a suitable girl for him to marry. A matchmaker sorted out the details of the **dowry**. This dowry was a present of land or goods from the bride's father to her new husband. A priest advised on the best date for the wedding.

Babies

As soon as a baby was born, the parents went to see a priest. The priest told them what kind of life the baby would have, and the priest chose a lucky day on which to name the baby.

Children's toys
Aztec boys played with tiny bows and arrows, shields, and spears. They played with small tools of their father's craft or trade. Aztec girls played with tiny spindles for spinning thread, brooms, and cooking pots. These toys helped boys and girls learn the things they needed to know when they were adults.

GROWING UP AND GOING TO SCHOOL

At home, children learned the things they would need to do when they were grown up. Boys helped their fathers farm and fish. Girls helped their mothers spin, weave, cook, and clean.

Boys' schools

Boys had to go to school. Most boys went to a **telpochcalli**. This was a school run by their calpulli. They learned how to fight and how to farm. Boys from noble families went to a temple school, the **calmecac**. They learned how to become judges, generals, priests, or government officials.

Aztec parents teaching young children
The fathers on the left of the picture are teaching their sons. The blue circles show that one son is three years old and the other son is four. The mothers on the right of the picture are teaching their daughters.

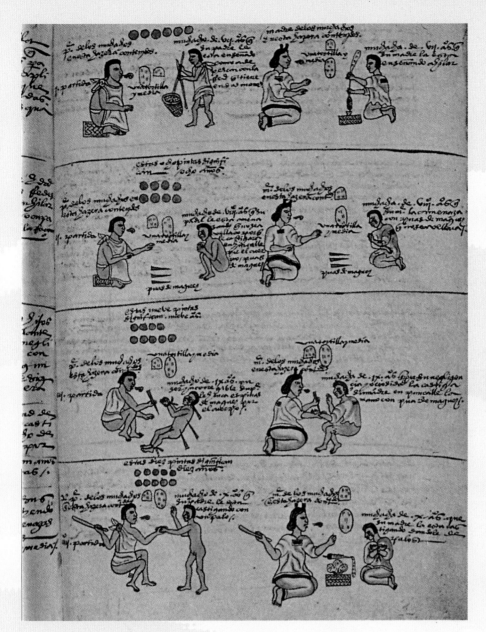

Girls' schools

Girls did not have to go to school. The daughters of nobles could go to a calmecac if their parents wanted them to. At the calmecac, the noble's daughters learned how to be priestesses and healers.

WHAT DID THE AZTECS BELIEVE?

Aztecs worshipped many different gods. They believed that the gods controlled everything in their lives and everything that grew on the earth. It was important to keep the gods happy. The Aztecs did this by having religious ceremonies for almost everything that happened in their lives.

Life after death

The Aztecs believed that people lived on when their life on Earth was over. The type of afterlife they had depended on the way they had lived in this life. For example, a brave soldier would travel around the earth for four years and then return to the earth as a hummingbird. A woman who died in childbirth would become a goddess. When someone died, their family dressed them in their best clothes. The family danced and chanted funeral prayers for four days. Then the Aztec's body was buried or cremated. If cremated, the ashes were buried with the Aztec's possessions and enough food for the long journey to the **underworld**.

Household gods
Every home had statues of the gods that were specially worshipped by the family that lived there.

The Aztec gods

The Aztecs believed that the gods lived above the dirt in 13 layers of heaven. The most powerful gods lived in the very top layer.

The most important god was called Huitzilopochtli. He was the Sun God and the God of War. Aztecs thought that if they didn't please Huitzilopochtli, the Sun would no longer shine and the world would be in darkness. They worshipped the Sun god by sacrificing people and offering their blood to the Sun. Aztecs believed the Sun needed human blood to give it strength and to keep it moving across the sky.

The god Quetzalcoatl looked after learning and schools. He was also the God of the Wind who made new life.

Chalchihuitlicue was the Water Goddess. She was married to Tlaloc, the God of Rain.

A mask of the god Quetzalcoatl
It is decorated with the precious stone turquoise.

A mask of the goddess Chalchihuitlicue

CEREMONIES AND TEMPLES

Ceremonies

The Aztecs had important religious ceremonies every few weeks. Most of the ceremonies had to do with farming. Aztecs prayed to Tlaloc, the Rain God, and to the goddesses of water, corn, and land.

The Aztecs believed that their gods wanted human blood and that the Sun would not rise in the morning without it. Aztec priests sacrificed many men, women, and children in their temples. The priest held a victim down, facing upwards, on a special stone. Then another priest cut open the person's chest. The heart was held up to the Sun and then put in a sacred dish. Most people were probably willing to die like this. They were sure they would go straight to the highest heaven.

Not all the Aztec ceremonies took place every day or even every year. Aztecs believed that one age ended and another began every 52 years. They made special sacrifices to please the gods and to ensure the beginning of a new age.

A carving of a man carrying a cocoa pod
This man is offering a cocoa pod to the gods. Many boys became priests when they grew up. Priests taught in the schools, organized religious ceremonies, kept the fires burning in the temples, and made sacrifices to the gods.

Temples

There were many temples in every city. The Aztecs built their temples by first making huge mounds of earth. Then they covered the mounds with mud bricks or stone. They built hundreds of steps into the sides of these pyramid shapes. The priests and their sacrifices used the steps to climb to the top. At the top of each pyramid, the Aztecs built a temple. The temples were on the top in order to be near the gods. They were also on the top so that everyone could watch the actions of the priests.

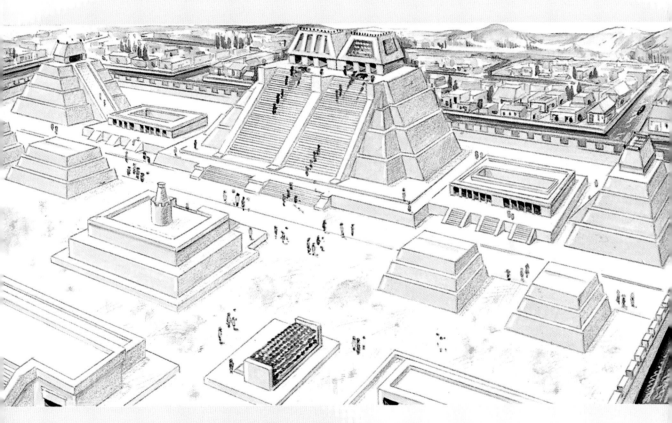

The great temple and square in Tenochtitlan
This is a modern drawing. We know the great temple and square in Tenochtitlan probably looked like this, because the Spaniards wrote detailed descriptions of Tenochtitlan. Archaeologists have found much of the remaining city and confirmed the writings.

THE AZTEC CALENDAR

It was important to the Aztecs that they had an accurate calendar. They needed to know when to plant their crops and when to harvest them. They needed to know when to hold their religious ceremonies. They thought that certain days were unlucky for events such as expeditions or wars. The Aztecs had two calendars. One, the Sun Calendar, was very much like ours. Aztecs used it to determine the seasons of the year. The other, the Sacred Calendar, was important for the priests and **astrologers**.

The Aztec Sun Calendar
This Calendar Stone was carved by the Aztecs, probably in the 1470s.
When the Spaniards came, the stone was lost for 200 years. Then it was
accidentally dug up in 1790. The Sun God is in the middle of the stone.

A carving showing the "tying up of the years"
The Aztecs believed that every 52 years one age ended and a new age began. The priests kept count by saving a reed each year. When they had 52 reeds, they tied them together and buried them, and a new age began.

The Sun Calendar

This calendar divided the year into 18 months and each month into 20 days. Our years have 365 days so there were five extra days in the haab (the Egyptian year). Aztecs said that these five days were unlucky. It was believed that babies born on these days would come to a bad end.

The Sacred Calendar

Aztecs called this calendar the **tonalpohualli**. This means the "Count of Days". The tonalpohualli divided the year into 260 days. Each day in the year had a different meaning. Priests and astrologers used this calendar to tell what would happen in the future and to decide the lucky and the unlucky days.

The Count of Days
Each day from 1 to 20 had a glyph to describe it. These are some of them.

THE CITY OF TENOCHTITLAN

The Aztecs built their first temple on an island in the middle of a swampy lake. A city grew up around this temple. The Aztecs called this city Tenochtitlan, which means "The Place of the Fruit of the Prickly Pear Cactus".

Building the city

The Aztecs were very good engineers. They built three **causeways** over the swamp to link the city with the mainland. There were bridges in the causeways that could be taken down to leave gaps and stop enemies from entering the city. The engineers built stone **aqueducts** to bring fresh water from the mainland to the city.

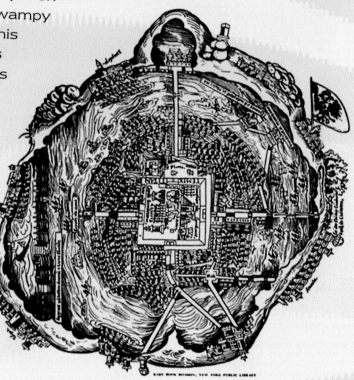

A plan of Tenochtitlan
This plan was drawn by Cortés when the Spaniards invaded. You can see the main square in the middle with the temple on one side of the square.

Inside the city

By 1519, about 200,000 people lived in Tenochtitlan. The houses had only one storey and a flat roof. In the middle of the city was a large square. In the square was the emperor's palace and the great temple. There were not many roads. People travelled in canoes along the canals that linked all parts of the city.

24

The lake city of Tenochtitlan
This is a modern drawing of Tenochtitlan. How do you think the artist knew what to draw?

FLOATING GARDENS

Tenochtitlan stood on an island in the middle of the swampy Lake Texcoco. Lake Texcoco was linked to four other shallow, swampy lakes. The land around them could get very dry when there was little rain.

The Aztecs drained parts of Lake Texcoco. On the drained land they made thousands of swamp gardens called **chinampas**. The gardens were linked by water. The water was used to **irrigate** the gardens.

The maguey cactus plant
This is a photograph of the maguey cactus plant. Aztecs used nearly every part of it. They used its spines as needles and for pricking children when they were naughty. They spun cactus fibres together to make thread, which they wove into cloth. The pulp was made into a drink called pulque. It was used as medicine.

Feeding the people

As Tenochtitlan grew, the Aztecs drained more and more land.
Farmers had only hoes and digging sticks, but the land was very
fertile and crops grew easily. The Aztecs grew corn, tomatoes,
beans, chili peppers, and prickly pears. They grew maguey cactus.
From the cactus they made a drink called pulque, and from its
fibres they wove cloth. They also grew cocoa trees. Aztecs used
cocoa beans for trading and to make a chocolate drink.

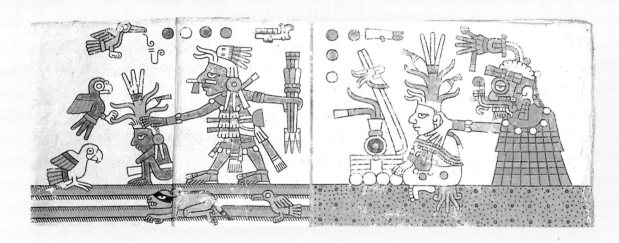

The life of a corn plant

*Corn was so important to the Aztecs that special gods and goddesses were
in charge of it. On the right of the first picture, Tlaloc, the Rain God, pours
water on the plant. In the second year, on the left, there is no rain. Xipe
Xiuhtecuhtli, the God of Planting and the Spring, is in charge. The soil is
hard and the plants cannot take root. They are attacked by birds. In the
third year, on the right of the second picture, the Storm Goddess pours
water onto a strong, young plant. The fourth year, on the left, is bad again.*

AZTEC HOMES

There were big differences between the homes of rich Aztecs and the homes of poor Aztecs.

Poor Aztecs lived on the edge of Tenochtitlan. Their houses were made from reeds that were woven together and then plastered with mud. They usually had just one room.

Richer Aztecs, such as craft workers, lived closer to the centre of Tenochtitlan. Their houses were built from **adobe** bricks made from mud. They had several rooms that opened on to a central courtyard.

Most families had a separate, outside bathhouse. Many families raised turkeys for meat and eggs and kept beehives for honey.

Nobles lived in the middle of Tenochtitlan. Their palaces were built from beautifully carved stone. Many of the palaces had more than 100 rooms. Their courtyards were filled with flowers. The grand houses and palaces were whitewashed so that they gleamed in the sun.

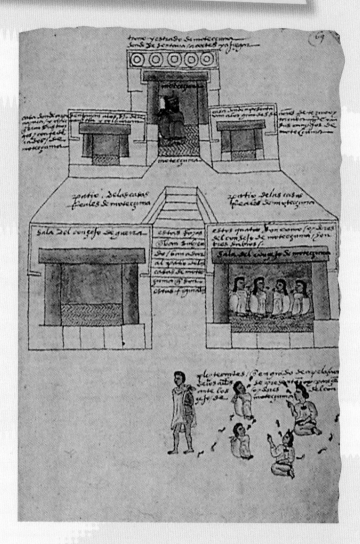

The king's palace
This Aztec drawing gives us some idea of what Moctezuma's palace looked like. It was almost like a small town. You can see the Emperor Moctezuma on the top floor in the middle of the picture. This was where he lived. On the ground floor there were council offices, law courts, and store rooms for tributes.

Inside an Aztec home

Aztecs did not have much furniture. Everyone slept on woven mats that were spread on the floor at night. During the day they sat on large cushions filled with straw. Families had cooking pots and storage jars made from clay, as well as grinding stones for grinding corn into flour. Every home had a special **shrine** for their household god.

Inside an Aztec house
Can you tell whether this is the house of a wealthy or a poor Aztec family?

A priest's house in Teotihuacan
This is a photograph of a house that was built at the same time as the Aztecs built theirs. It is probably similar to the houses in which Aztec nobles lived.

COOKING AND EATING

Aztec wives spent their time cooking, weaving, and looking after their children. Even the wives of nobles were expected to be good cooks so that they could organize their servants.

Everyday food

Corn was the Aztecs' main food. The women ground it into flour and made **tortillas**. They made a porridge from corn. This was called **atolli**. Sometimes they added honey or chilies to the atolli.

Aztecs ate a lot of beans. The women usually boiled them and flavoured them with tomatoes and chilies. They gathered wild fruit and vegetables, such as figs and nuts, to add to their meals.

Turkeys and dogs were the only animals the Aztecs raised for food. They hunted for any other meat they wanted. Aztecs trapped rabbits and deer and netted the wild ducks that flew over the lakes. They fished in the lakes for turtles, newts, salamanders, frogs, tadpoles, and shellfish.

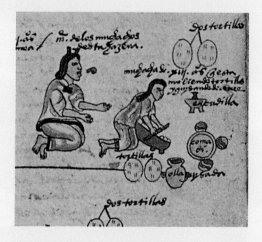

Grinding corn
*In the top picture a mother is teaching her daughter how to grind corn to make flour. The girl is using a roller made of stone, called a **metate**, to crush the grains. The metate was rolled up and down a block of stone called a **mano**. In the bottom picture Aztecs are storing grain in pots. Pots like these are still used in Mexico.*

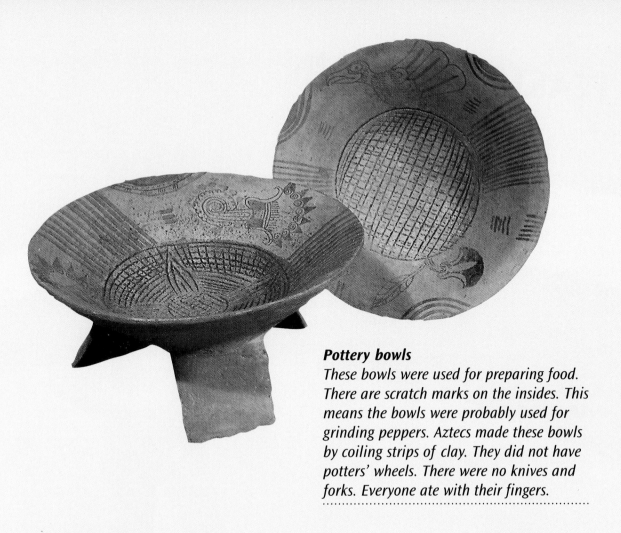

Pottery bowls

These bowls were used for preparing food. There are scratch marks on the insides. This means the bowls were probably used for grinding peppers. Aztecs made these bowls by coiling strips of clay. They did not have potters' wheels. There were no knives and forks. Everyone ate with their fingers.

Special food

On special occasions, Aztec commoners might roast a duck, turkey, rabbit, or dog. Rich Aztecs ate this type of food all the time, as well as roast pheasants and wild pigs. When rich Aztecs had special feasts, they ate roast quail, pigeons, geese, pelicans, and cranes. Most people drank pulque. However, the nobles' favourite drink was **chocolatl** made from cocoa beans. They crushed the beans and made a frothy drink flavoured with vanilla and spices.

A hairless dog
This is a pottery model of an Aztec hairless dog. Aztecs raised these dogs to roast and eat.

FEASTS AND FUN

The wealthy nobles in Tenochtitlan often held large feasts. Their houses were scented with perfumes of herbs and flowers. Their servants served food to the guests. The guests ate with their fingers, but washed their hands before and after the feast. They smoked tobacco in pipes or cigars. They crushed dried tobacco leaves to make **snuff**. Women went to these banquets, but no one knows whether they smoked.

Food for the Emperor

When the Emperor Moctezuma had a feast, there were more than 100 different types of food for the guests to eat. There were roast meats in different sauces. There were many kinds of vegetables and fruit. The cooks made sweet pastries from corn flour and sugar.

The tables were decorated with gold and silver vases. Cups and spoons were made from gold, silver, and tortoiseshell. The spoons were just for serving. Everyone ate with their fingers.

The Aztecs were good dancers
This is a pottery model of a trained dancer and singer. He is wearing a loin cloth, which he holds with one hand. He is also wearing lip and ear jewellery.

Music and dancing

After feasts, the Aztecs danced. Orchestras played drums, rattles, flutes, whistles, and trumpets made from shells.

Ceremonies and festivals for the gods always included singing and dancing. Every temple had a **tlapizcatzin** who trained singers. Singers and dancers were very important to the Aztecs.

An Aztec drum
The outside of this drum is made of carved wood. On top are two flaps of wood that made different musical notes when struck by the drummer. The Aztecs called this kind of two-tone drum a teponaztli.

A pottery whistle
Musicians played small whistles like this. They also played pottery flutes and rattles made from hollowed-out gourds.

SPORTS AND GAMES

Sports

Aztec nobles played a game called **tlachtli**. They played it at special times, such as at religious festivals. Two teams played on a stone court surrounded by stone walls. To score, one team had to get a small rubber ball through a stone ring set high in the wall. The players were only allowed to touch the ball with their knees, elbows, or hips. Players were often hurt and sometimes killed. Everyone came to watch and cheer for their team.

A tlachtli court
This is a photograph of a tlachtli court at Chichen Itza. Mayans, Toltecs, and Aztecs played tlachtli. They played it with a ball made from the sap of rubber trees that grow wild in the South American rainforests.

Games

All Aztecs played a game called **patolli**. They tossed a number cube and moved coloured beans on a board until they got three beans in a row. Aztecs held patolli competitions. Some Aztecs bet on the games. A Spanish writer tells how people sometimes lost their homes, their fields, their corn granaries, and their cactus plants. Then they and their families had to become slaves.

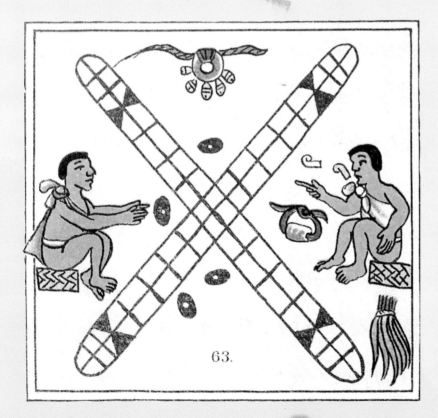

63.

A patolli game
We know about patolli from Aztec pictures like this and from Spanish writers. A Spanish writer named Duran wrote that good players carried their own game mats with them. They also carried their own game pieces tied up in small cloths.

CRAFTS AND TRADES

Many Aztecs were craft workers. Stoneworkers, carpenters, potters, mat and basket workers, and weavers made everyday objects. Feather workers, metalworkers, sculptors, jewellers, and painters made luxury objects.

Feather workers

It took years to learn to be a feather worker. Parents taught their children the feather workers' skills. Some of the skills are shown here.

First the pattern was designed. Then the children mixed the glues while the men prepared the cotton backing. The cotton was glued and reglued until it was stiff and shiny. The design was traced on the cotton. The women prepared the feathers, which came from colourful birds such as quetzals and parrots.

Guilds

Craft workers lived and worked in separate areas of Aztec cities. They worshipped their own gods. Usually whole families worked at the same craft. Families who lived in the same calpulli were able to organize **guilds** and train **apprentices**.

Craftworkers

Aztecs did not use wheels. They did not use carts or pulleys to carry and lift raw materials such as stone, wood, and metal. Slaves did this work. Aztecs did not have iron to make knives, chisels, or other tools. They used blades made from a mixture of copper and tin to cut and carve stone and wood. Aztec potters did not use potters' wheels. They made coil pots and then smoothed the clay until no bumps remained.

Feather workers, goldsmiths, silversmiths, jewellers, and painters worked only for the nobility. They made gold nose and lip jewellery. They used precious stones, such as rubies, to make necklaces and bracelets.

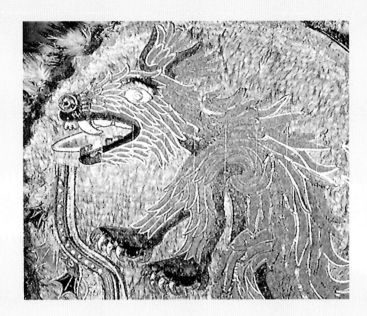

A feather-work shield
This shield was made by feather workers. The feathers were glued to cotton that had been stretched over a wooden frame.

A turquoise ornament
This ornament is made from gold and decorated with a stone called turquoise. A nobleman would have worn this on his chest. Aztec craftworkers made jewellery and other ornaments.

BUYING AND SELLING

Every village, town, and city in the Aztec Empire had an open-air market. Most markets were open five days a week. People went there to buy and sell. They also went there to meet their friends.

Bartering

Aztecs did not use money. They bought and sold goods by barter. They swapped what they had to sell for goods of the same value. The value of goods was carefully worked out. Everything, whether gold, corn, or a slave, could be valued in cocoa beans or cotton cloaks called **quachtli**.

The market at Tenochtitlan

Every day a great market was held in the centre of Tenochtitlan. Thousands of people came from all over the Aztec Empire to buy and sell goods. They brought expensive items such as golden goblets and jade necklaces. They brought ordinary things such as black beans and pottery dishes. They brought slaves, puppies, and salt. Officials made sure that the buyers and sellers did not cheat or charge prices that were too high.

Beautiful jewellery, such as this jade serpent, was traded at the great market at Tenochtitlan.

Aztec prices

The Aztecs measured the price of something by how many cloaks (quachtli) or how many cocoa beans it was worth. Here are some examples:

1 dugout canoe = 1 cloak

1 slave = 25 cloaks

1 feather cape = 100 cloaks

The market at Tenochtitlan

This is a modern reconstruction of the Aztec market at Tenochtitlan. The sellers spread out what they had to sell on mats. They sat on the ground and waited for buyers. Vegetables were sold in one part of the market, pottery in another, and so on. There were no shops, so people had to buy everything they needed in the markets.

AZTEC MERCHANTS

Merchants, called **pochteca** by the Aztecs, travelled the entire Aztec Empire and far beyond it. They looked for goods to buy and bring back to the cities. They looked for gold, silver, copper, and precious stones for the craft workers. The craft workers depended on the merchants for the materials they needed. The merchants took with them luxury goods such as gold necklaces, ruby earrings, and **obsidian** razors to sell far and wide.

Merchants travelled in groups with porters to carry the heavy things. They only travelled on especially lucky days. They kept their trading details secret. They returned to their cities at night and immediately hid their goods.

Aztec merchants
These pictures are from an Aztec codex. The merchant is in the right-hand picture. He is carrying quetzal feathers on his back. Merchants had their own god, Yacatecuhtli. Yacatecuhtli is in the left-hand picture carrying a crossroads sign on his back. A footprint was the Aztec glyph for a journey. Can you find the footprints in this picture?

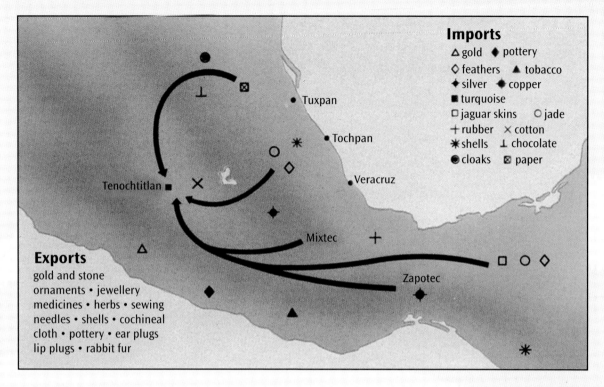

Imports
△ gold ◆ pottery
◇ feathers ▲ tobacco
✦ silver ◆ copper
■ turquoise
□ jaguar skins ○ jade
+ rubber × cotton
✳ shells ⊥ chocolate
● cloaks ⊠ paper

Tuxpan

Tochpan

Veracruz

Tenochtitlan

Mixtec

Zapotec

Exports
gold and stone
ornaments • jewellery
medicines • herbs • sewing
needles • shells • cochineal
cloth • pottery • ear plugs
lip plugs • rabbit fur

Aztec trading
This map shows where the Aztecs
traded. The key tells the goods
that they bought and sold.

Merchant guilds

Merchants were important people. They had their
own guild and their own law courts. They could own
land. They were allowed to send their children to the
calmecac with the nobles' children. The government
was in charge of all trading and shared in the profits
from the goods the merchants brought back.

Merchant spies

Merchants travelled far and wide. Some of them
brought back information for the emperor. They told
him about plots in far-away towns. They told him
about strangers who had arrived in the Aztec Empire.

TRAVEL AND TRANSPORT

The Aztecs never discovered that wheels could be used to move things, so they did not have carts and wagons.

There were no horses, donkeys, or oxen in the entire Aztec Empire. This meant that the Aztecs could not use animals as pack animals to carry their goods. Everything carried over land was carried on the backs of porters, who were sometimes slaves.

Difficult journeys

Some overland journeys were very difficult. They were made by merchants who travelled across mountain ranges, through steaming jungles, and over sandy plains. They travelled in groups called **caravans**.

Sometimes soldiers went with the caravans to guard them. Merchants and soldiers were the only Aztecs who travelled long distances. Nobles travelled between Tenochtitlan and their lands in the country, but these were not long journeys.

Merchants carrying weapons
These Aztec pictures tell us that Aztec merchants carried weapons when they travelled. Why do you think they needed to do this?

The volcano of Popacatapetl
This photograph of the volcano Popacatapetl gives us an idea of what the Aztec countryside looked like. It must have been difficult for merchants to make long journeys on foot over land like this.

Canals and waterways

Most Aztecs used flat-bottomed wooden boats and canoes to travel around Technotitlan and out to their fields.

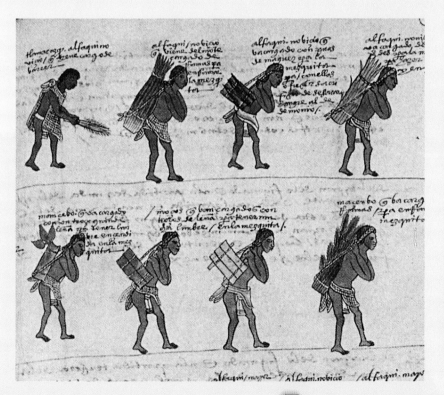

Aztec porters
These Aztec pictures show porters carrying trading goods for the merchants. Each porter carried between 20 and 30 kilograms (40–70 pounds) on his back. Do you see the strap going around their foreheads? How would this make it easier to carry heavy goods?

EARLY HISTORY

Most of the Aztecs' early history is based on legends. One legend says that long ago they left an island home called Aztlan. This was because their priests told them that the god Huitzilopochtli would make them lords of the world.

The Aztecs' wanderings
The Aztecs would have wandered through country like this on their journey from Aztlan to the Valley of Mexico.

The Hill of the Locust

The Valley of Mexico was already divided into **city-states** when the Aztecs arrived. The Aztecs tried to take over some farmland, but other tribes drove them away. In 1299 they arrived at Chapultepec, "The Hill of the Locust." The Aztecs settled here and began to farm. However, within 20 years, the other tribes drove them out to the shores of Lake Texcoco.

Fighting for land

The Aztecs fled to Culhuacan on the other side of the lake. The Culhua people forced the Aztecs to live on dry and barren land, hoping they would die there. The Aztecs, however, did well and soon wanted more land. They had to fight the Culhua for this. Eventually the Aztecs fled to an island in the middle of Lake Texcoco. On the island, the Aztecs found a cactus with an eagle perched on it. The eagle was carrying a snake in its beak. This is what the god Huitzilopochtli had told them to look for. They knew they had to build a city there, and Huitzilopochtli would make them lords of the world.

The Aztecs settle
This is a picture from an Aztec codex. It shows the beginnings of Tenochtitlan. In the middle is the cactus with the eagle perched on top. Can you find the lake and the four quarters of the city the Aztecs were going to build?

BUILDING AN EMPIRE

The first Aztec ruler in Tenochtitlan was Tenoc. He made peace with the Culhua people. A Culhua named Acamapichtli became the next ruler of the Aztecs. The **alliance** with the Culhua gave the Aztecs more power. However, the Tepaneca tribe was still the most powerful in the valley. They seized city-states and began to build an empire. The Aztecs quickly made an alliance with them.

Itzcoatl

The Aztecs gain power

In 1426, the Aztecs had a new leader, Itzcoatl. Under him, the Aztecs allied with the people in the cities of Texcoco and Tlacoan. Together, in 1428, they defeated the Tepaneca and captured their capital city.

The Aztec Empire grows

Itzcoatl died in 1440. His nephew, Moctezuma I, became emperor. Moctezuma wanted to make the Aztec Empire bigger by conquering lands outside the valley. However, he had bad luck.

Ahuitzotl

The Aztec rulers

Acamapichtli	(1372–1391)
Huitzilhuitl	(1391–1415)
Chimalpopoca	(1415–1426)
Itzcoatl	(1426–1440)
Moctezuma I	(1440–1468)
Axayacatl	(1468–1481)
Tizoc	(1481–1486)
Ahuitzotl	(1486–1502)
Moctezuma II	(1502–1520)

Moctezuma II

In 1446, Tenochtitlan was badly flooded. Then there were years of bad harvests and famine. Thousands of Aztecs died. Moctezuma was determined that this would not happen again. He set out to conquer wealthy lands where there was good farmland. The Aztecs did not settle on these conquered lands. They let the lords stay in control as long as they paid tributes to the Aztecs.

The Aztec Empire was large and powerful when Moctezuma died in 1468. In 1502, when the ruler Ahuitzotl died, the nobles chose his nephew, Moctezuma II, to rule. He was to make the Aztec empire even greater.

The Stone of Tizoc
This is a carving showing the great deeds of Tizoc, an Aztec king. Can you see him holding the hair of a prisoner?

AZTEC WARRIORS

The Aztecs were ruthless warriors.
They built up an empire because of their
fighting skills.

A successful warrior

Most boys wanted to be warriors. Young boys were
trained to fight. They were taught how to take
prisoners. When a boy was 10 years old, his hair was
cut, leaving a lock of hair at the back of his neck.
This lock was cut off when the boy took his first
prisoner. When he had captured or killed four prisoners,
he was allowed to wear a special cape and join in
battle discussions. After that, he could become a
tlacateccatl, or commander.

*Dressing
for battle*
*War lords and
knights wore
splendid uniforms
covered with
feather work. The
type and colour
of the feathers
showed a soldier's
rank. For example,
a captain always
wore red feathers.*

The Aztec army

The Aztecs had an army of full-time professional soldiers. The best fighters became eagle knights and wore eagle's head helmets in battle, or they became jaguar knights and wore jaguar skins in battle. Under them came thousands of ordinary warriors.

All Aztec men, except slaves, had to do military service and learn how to fight. When there was a war, all the calpullis had to send as many men as possible to fight. They were organized into companies of 200 to 400 men. The companies were grouped into larger regiments. Every regiment was commanded by a professional soldier.

Aztec warriors fought with spears and **javelins** that could be thrown a great distance. Some Aztecs fought with wooden sticks edged with sharpened obsidian. They wore armour made of cotton that was padded to make it thicker and then soaked in salt water. This made the cotton stiff so that it could not be easily pierced. Warriors carried shields covered in animal skin and decorated with feathers.

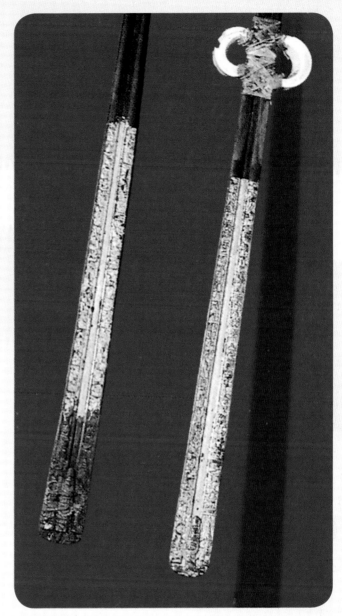

A spear thrower
Warriors hurled spears and javelins with these spear throwers. The spear fitted into a groove and was held by a hook. A warrior could throw a spear at great speed using a spear thrower. The Aztecs called a spear thrower an atlatl.

AZTEC WARFARE

Aztec rulers would start a battle for almost any reason, for example, if someone had insulted them, or if a city had not paid its tribute.

Planning the attack

Aztecs did not launch surprise attacks. First, they sent nobles to the city they planned to attack. The nobles asked the city's leader to join the Aztecs. The city had 20 days to decide. Aztec nobles would visit the city twice more, and each time they threatened and warned. If, finally, the city would not agree to pay tribute to the Aztecs, war was declared. The Aztecs, meanwhile, had plenty of time to scout the land.

Huitzilopochtli, the Sun God and the God of War
Aztecs took as many prisoners as possible so they could sacrifice them to Huitzilopochtli. They took the prisoners away in long lines with their hands tied behind them and their necks in wooden collars.

A prisoner
This prisoner is being threatened by four jaguar knights. If he defeated all four knights, the Aztecs would let him live. If not, he would be sacrificed.

Medicine and healing

An Aztec who was ill visited a **diviner**. The diviner threw corn seeds on to a mat. He could tell what the illness was by looking at the pattern made by the seeds. The ill person then went to see a **ticitl**, who was a doctor. The ticitl knew how to use more than 130 herbs to make different kinds of medicines. Ticitl used mushrooms, and they gave patients steam baths to sweat a fever out.

Some ticitl accompanied the Aztec armies into battle. They set broken bones and used different mixtures to treat wounds.

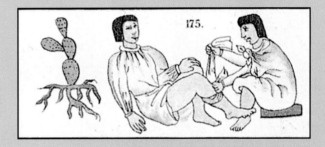

These two pictures show the ticitl at work.

Launching the attack

Aztec leaders organized the army. Warriors came from all over the empire to fight the enemy. Priests decided on a lucky day to fight the battle.

The battle was usually short and fierce. Aztecs did not try to kill enemy soldiers. They tried to take them prisoner so that they could sacrifice them later. If the Aztecs won, they decided on the tribute the defeated city had to pay. Aztecs burned the enemy's temples and made the defeated people worship the Aztec god Huitzilopochtli.

MOCTEZUMA THE EMPEROR

Moctezuma became emperor in 1502. Tenochtitlan was a huge city. Most, but not all, of the neighbouring cities were part of the Aztec Empire. The land around them belonged to the empire. Conquering new lands meant longer and longer journeys. The warriors began to complain.

A new idea

Moctezuma decided to try something different. He attacked the nearby city-states that were not part of the empire.

Moctezuma wearing his royal robes
A nobleman is helping Moctezuma put on his headdress. Moctezuma is wearing nose and ear jewellery.

The ashen bird
Aztecs said that when this bird appeared, something evil was going to happen. In an Aztec story, fishermen brought this bird to Moctezuma. He looked into the mirror on the bird's crest and saw warriors riding on deer.

The Spanish arrive

While the fighting was going on, Moctezuma faced new and frightening events.

For several years the Aztecs received **omens** that something evil was going to happen. Some Aztecs saw tongues of fire in the skies; some saw Lake Texcoco boil; others said that lightning struck a temple and a shrine burst into flames. Suddenly messengers began arriving in Tenochtitlan with strange tales. They said that white-skinned men with beards had arrived on the east coast and were travelling through Maya country. They were getting closer and closer to Tenochtitlan. Moctezuma remembered an old Aztec legend. The god Quetzalcoatl had long ago vanished across the sea in the east. It was said that one day he would come back and claim his kingdom. The Aztecs were afraid. Were these white men from the east really gods? How could the Aztecs possibly fight a battle with gods? If they were men, what new weapons had they brought with them from across the sea?

Moctezuma goes to meet Cortés
This is a Spanish painting. It shows the Aztec emperor, Moctezuma, setting out to meet Hernan Cortés, the leader of the Spanish expedition. In what ways does Moctezuma look different here from the way he looks in Aztec paintings? Why do you think this is?

THE SPANISH CONQUISTADORS

In 1518, a Spanish captain named Juan de Grijalva led an expedition to the east coast of Mexico. While he was there, he met a tax collector called Pinotl who told him about an inland kingdom that owned plenty of gold. Grijalva took this information back to Spain. A new expedition was organized. The commander was soldier and explorer Hernan Cortés.

The Aztecs meet Cortés

In 1519, Cortés and his men landed at Veracruz. Quickly, Moctezuma made plans. He sent priests and warriors to meet the **conquistadors** at Veracruz. They took precious gifts for the men they thought were gods. Cortés challenged Moctezuma's men to fight, but the Aztecs were afraid and fled to Tenochtitlan. Moctezuma was puzzled. He sent more gifts. He watched and waited. Meanwhile, Cortés and his men began to march towards Tenochtitlan. Before they left Veracruz, they burned the boats that had brought them. There was no going back.

A Spanish portrait of Hernan Cortés
This picture was painted when Cortés was about 34 years old. He is just about to set out on his expedition to Mexico.

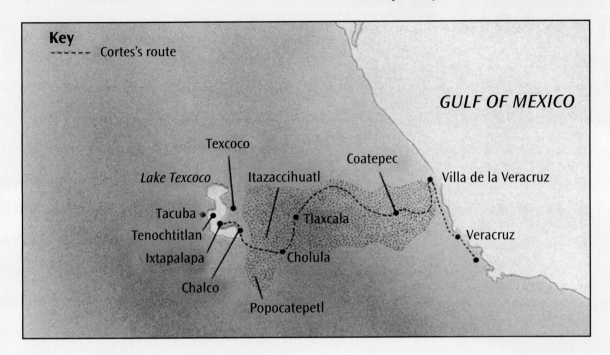

Key
- - - - - - Cortes's route

GULF OF MEXICO

Texcoco

Lake Texcoco

Itazaccihuatl

Coatepec

Villa de la Veracruz

Tacuba

Tenochtitlan

Tlaxcala

Veracruz

Ixtapalapa

Cholula

Chalco

Popocatepetl

Cortés marches to Tenochtitlan

No one really knows what Cortés was like. Some historians say he was a great general. Others say he was cunning and greedy for gold. We do know, however, that his men were ready to follow him through unknown lands and dangers.

Cortés and his army of 400 Spaniards began their march across mountainous country. When they reached Tlaxcala, high in the mountains, they were surrounded by thousands of warriors. Cortés had horses and guns, which the Tlaxcalans had never seen before. Cortés and his men won the battle. The Tlaxcalans agreed to join forces with Cortés against the Aztecs. Together they marched to Tenochtitlan.

Moctezuma's men met Cortés at Veracruz.
Moctezuma's men took gifts to Cortés. When they left, Cortés fired a gun. The Aztecs were very frightened.

THE FALL OF TENOCHTITLAN

Thousands of Aztecs watched as the conquistadors marched to Tenochtitlan. Moctezuma met them on a causeway outside the city. He welcomed them as if they were gods. He took them to a palace where they were to stay as honoured guests of the Aztecs.

The Spaniards were amazed when they saw the riches of Tenochtitlan. They decided they had to have it all for themselves. They invited Moctezuma to stay with them as a guest in their palace, but they treated him as a prisoner. He did all he could to please the Spaniards. Then Cortés began to complain about the statues of Aztec gods and their human sacrifices. Moctezuma was very angry.

The death of Moctezuma

Aztec warriors gathered in Tenochtitlan to celebrate the midsummer festival. A Spanish commander, Alvardo, thought they were going to attack the conquistadors. He ordered his men to kill them. However, the Aztecs fought back. As Moctezuma tried to calm them, he was killed.

Cortés speaking to Moctezuma
A woman called Dona Marina is helping Cortés understand what Moctezuma is saying. She spoke Nahuatl and Spanish.

The Aztecs imprisoning the Spaniards
The Aztecs at first treated the Spaniards like gods. Then, when Cortés took Moctezuma prisoner, the Aztecs realized that the Spanish were not to be trusted.

The Spaniards conquer Mexico
This is a Spanish painting. You can see the differences between Spanish and Aztec arms and armour. Do you think this meant that the Spaniards would win in the end?

Victory to the conquistadors

Cortés and his men fought their way out of Tenochtitlan. About 300 of them survived. Then they had to face a vast Aztec army at Otumba. The Aztecs tried to capture the Spaniards alive so they could sacrifice them later. The Spaniards concentrated on killing as many Aztecs as possible. The Spaniards won.

Other tribes quickly joined the Spaniards. They wanted to wipe out the hated Aztecs. Together they fought their way back up the causeways into Tenochtitlan. They **blockaded** the city so that no supplies could get in. Thousands of Aztecs died. The Spaniards finally captured the city in April 1521. The Aztec Empire was gone forever.

NEW SPAIN

The Aztecs were defeated because they were fighting an enemy they did not understand. They fought to please the gods and take captives. The Spaniards fought with superior weapons and tried to kill the Aztec commanders first so there would be no one to give orders to the Aztec warriors.

Spanish rule

Ten years after the conquest, all of Mexico was under Spanish rule. It was called New Spain, and Cortés was made governor. Spanish settlers made the Aztecs work for them. In return, they converted them to Christianity. The Aztecs became slaves to the Spaniards.

Aztecs at a Christian religious service
After the Spaniards had conquered the Aztecs, Christian missionaries arrived in Mexico. The Spaniards thought they were making things better for the Aztecs by converting them to Christianity, and by teaching them to read, write, and work in the European way. In fact, they were destroying the Aztecs' way of life.

The ruins of Moctezuma's summer palace
The Spaniards tore down Tenochtitlan. They destroyed everything. They melted down the gold objects. Some things were sent to Spain and these have survived. The only other artefacts not destroyed were buried under the ruins of Tenochtitlan. They are still being uncovered by archaeologists.

Thousands of Aztecs died because of the way the Spaniards treated them. They died from accidents, overwork, and pneumonia. Thousands more died from the European diseases the Spaniards brought with them: smallpox, measles, chicken pox, and typhus.

The legacy of the Aztecs

The Spaniards ruled in New Spain until 1821. The Aztecs were forced to give up their lands and their way of life. Today there are only about 3,000 Aztecs in Mexico. They still speak Nahuatl and hold some of the Aztec festivals, but these are mainly for tourists.

The flag of Mexico
The modern flag of Mexico has the Aztec eagle and cactus in the centre.

TIMELINE

BC

1300	Olmec civilization in Mexico

AD

300–900	Maya civilization in Yucatan
900–1150	Toltec empire in Mexico
1111	Aztecs leave Aztlan
1299	Aztecs arrive at Chapultepec
1319	Aztecs flee to Culhuacan
1325	Aztecs build Tenochtitlan
1440	Moctezuma I becomes emperor
1502	Moctezuma II becomes emperor
1518	Moctezuma hears about white men in Mexico
1519	Cortés' fleet lands at Veracruz
1520	Moctezuma killed
1521	Fall of Tenochtitlan
1531	Mexico comes under Spanish rule and is called New Spain
1821	End of Spanish rule in Mexico

PRONUNCIATION OF AZTEC WORDS

Aztec word	Pronunciation
Acamapichtli	A-kama-pich-tlee
calpulli	kal-pulee
Chalchihuitlicue	Chal-chi-hooit-licoo
chocolatl	choko-latel
Ehecatl-Quetzalcoatl	E-ekatel/Ket-sal-koatel
Huitzilopochtli	Wit-thil-o-poch-tlee
maguey	mag-oo-ay
Nahuatl	Na-wa-tel
patolli	pat-olee
pochteca	poch-teka
Popacatapetl	Popa-kata-petel
pulque	pul-k
quachtli	kach-tlee
Quetzalcoatl	Ket-sal-koatel
Tenochtitlan	Ten-och-tit-lan
teponaztli	te-pon-ath-tlee
ticitl	tik-i-tel
tlachtli	tlach-tlee
Tlalacel	Tlal-a-kel
Tlaloc	Tlal-ok
tlapizcatzin	tla-pith-cat-thin
tlatocan	tlat-o-kan
Tochtepec	Toch-te-pek
tonalpohualli	tonal-pok-ooal-ee
tortilla	tort-ee-ya
Xipe	Shipe
Xiuhtecuhtli	Sheoo-te-kutlee

GLOSSARY

adobe sun-dried mud bricks

alliance union or friendly agreement between two countries or states by which they become allies

amatl type of paper made from bark

apprentice person who learns a craft or trade by working for a skilled craft worker

aqueduct channel made by people for carrying water across a valley

archaeologist person who studies what happened in the past by finding and examining old buildings and objects

artefact object made by people in the past

astrologer person who studies the stars

atolli type of corn porridge eaten by the Aztecs

blockade to surround a place with the goal of starving the people trapped inside and forcing them to surrender

calmecac Aztec temple school for the sons of nobles

calpulli group of Aztec families who owned land that was farmed by those families and run by a calpullec or headman

caravan group of merchants travelling together for safety

causeway raised roadway across water

chinampa Aztec floating garden

chocolatl Aztec drink made from cocoa beans

city-state city that is also an independent state with its own rulers

civilization large group of people who have settled in one place and live in the same organized way, following the same customs and creating their own style in art

codex Aztec book of picture symbols (the plural of codex is codices)

conquistadors Spanish conquerors

council group of people who are in charge of the day-to-day organization of a town or city

diviner person who claims to be able to see the future by using magic

dowry money given by a bride's father to a bridegroom

empire group of countries or states ruled by one king or queen who may be called an emperor or empress

excavate to carefully dig up buried objects to find out about the past

glyph picture symbol standing for a word or idea

guild society of people in the same trade

irrigate to water crops by channelling water from a river or lake along pipes or ditches

javelin type of spear, usually thrown

loin cloth cloth that covers the loins, the part of the body between the waist and thighs

mano block of stone on which grain was laid to be crushed with a metate

merchant person who buys goods in one place and sells them somewhere else, often in a different country

metate roller made of stone used to crush grain

noble person born into an important family; the group of nobles in one country is called the nobility

obsidian dark, shiny type of rock that comes from volcanoes

omen unusual happening or sign that some people believe means something is about to happen

patolli game played on a board with coloured stones and a number cube

pochteca merchant

quachtli cotton cloak worn by Aztecs

scribe person who wrote out documents and books by hand

sculptor artist who makes statues or other objects from stone or metals

shrine altar or small chapel to a god or saint

slave person who is owned by a master and has to work without pay

snuff kind of tobacco that is not smoked but sniffed through the nose

telpochcalli school for the sons of Aztec commoners

temple building or place where people worshipped their gods

ticitl Aztec doctor

tlacateccatl commander of Aztec warriors

tlachtli ball game played in ancient Mexico

tlapizcatzin caretaker of an Aztec temple

tlatocan large council that advised the Aztec king

tonalpohualli Aztec sacred calendar

tortilla flat bread made from corn flour

tribute type of tax paid in food and other goods

underworld place where the Aztecs believed people went when they died. It had nine layers and was ruled by gods.

Further reading

You can find out more about the Aztecs in books and on the Internet. Use a search engine such as www.yahooligans.com to search for information. A search for the word "Aztecs" will bring back lots of results, but it may be difficult to find the information you want. Try refining your search to look for some of the ideas mentioned in this book, such as "Aztec warfare."

More books to read
Aztecs, R. Thompson (Franklin Watts Ltd, 2003)
Aztecs and Maya, Fiona MacDonald (Southwater, 2001)

INDEX